Ordinary Women Engaged
In Extraordinary Work

A GUIDELINE MANUAL FOR STEWARDESSES
IN THE
AFRICAN METHODIST EPISCOPAL CHURCH

by

REV. RICHARD J. PARKER

AMEC Sunday School Union
Nashville, Tennessee

Any opinions and views expressed in this work are the author's own, and should not necessarily be considered as reflecting upon either the rubrics and/or the disciplines of the African Methodist Episcopal Church

---

Copyright © 1987 by Richard J. Parker

All rights reserved. No part of this publication may be reproduced, stored in a retrieval system, or transmitted in any form or by any means, electronics, mechanical, photocopying, recording or otherwise, except as may be expressly permitted by the 1976 Copyright Act or without the prior permission of the publisher. Requests for permission should be addressed in writing to Johnny Barbour, Jr., AMEC Sunday School Union, 500 Eighth Avenue South, Nashville, TN 37203-4181.

First printing, December 1991
ISBN: 0-929386-23-X

Library of Congress Catalog Card Number 91-77788

Manufactured by the AMEC Sunday School Union at
Nashville, Tennessee, United States of America.

Table of Contents

Preface ix

Preface (to Revised Edition) xiii

Section 1 -- The Stewardess Board

Purpose 3

Organization 4
    Multiple Boards   The Junior Board
    Officers and Committees   Acolytes

Outline of Duties 9
    Helpful Suggestions
    During Invitation
    At the Parsonage

Worship Attitudes and Ettiquette 13
    Standing
    Kneeling
    Bowing
    Walking
    Talking

The Stewardess Garb 14

Section 2 -- The Liturgical Symbols

Symbolism of Church Architecture 19

Altar and Chancel Appointments 25
    The Cross   The Baptismal Font
    The Candles   The Christian Flag
    The Paraments and   The Altar
        Linens

The Christian Year 28
The Seasons of the Church Year 30
 Advent   Eastertide
 Christmastide   Pentecost
 Epiphany   Kingdomtide
 Lent

Colors in the Church 31
 Purple   White
 Green   Black
 Red

Flowers in the Church 32

Section 3 -- The Sacraments

Holy Communion 40
 Preparations
 Worship Service Procedures
 For the Sick and Shut-In
 For the Bride and Groom

Recipe for Unleavened Bread 52

Holy Baptism 53
 Worship Service Procedures
  Sprinkling
  Pouring
  Immersion
  For the Sick and Shut-In

Section 4 -- The Celebrations

Weddings 59
 Flowers   Prayer Desk
 Aisle Cloth   Fasteners
 Candles

Home-Going (Funerals) 62
- Duties
  - Lying in State
  - Funeral Pall
  - Duties
  - Mourning Bows
  - Good Friday
  - Color
  - Candles
  - Chancel Metal Ware
  - Processional
  - During the Service
  - Recessional
  - At the Graveside
- Good Friday

Love Feast Celebration 70

Maundy Thursday Celebration 73
- Paschal Lamb Feast
- Prior preparations
- Menu Items
- Format

Section 5 -- Additional Information

Definitions of Ecclesiastical Terms 83

Reference Books for Further Reading 93

Appendices 95

Paschal Lamb Feast 97

New Stewardesses' Introduction Ceremony ... 99

Requirements / Equipment of the Sacristy 104

Care and Cleaning of Chancel Furnishings 108

Duty Checklist 113

Preface

*"Duty makes us do things well,
Love makes us do things beautifully."*

This manual is not to be considered a comprehensive, finished work, nor even the last word, in presenting the nature and the duties of the Stewardess Board in the African Methodist Episcopal Church (A.M.E.C.).

I have included, in my presentation what I learned long ago from my seminary texts and notes and the 28 years I have spent pastoring in the A.M.E. Church. During that time I spent two years in the foreign mission field of Bermuda, which exposed me to the European flavor of the Anglican Church, which Mothered the onset of Methodism. I was made quite vividly aware of their liturgical traditions and rubrics. I was also appointed for three years as a supply pastor in the United Methodist Church which has an excellent Altar Guild tradition. All of this reference material and personal, practical experience, has served me well in my research and editing, for the compiling of this manual.

I have not been able to find, in our own A.M.E. denominational printed materials, sufficient guidelines for much of our Worship practices. Therefore, in this manual I have sought to define what is thought to be necessary for the various Stewardess Boards, of the A.M.E. Church, to function in the most reverent, optimum, and efficient way possible.

Many aspects of our Worship Services are being robbed of their dignity by the rote mimicking we do of other denominational practices. Many of our own Pastors and Laity do not know, or seemingly don't even care to know, of our own traditions which have been our heritage and legacy even down to this Bicentennial year.

Present day worship, so-called, is more like entertainment, rather than the worship of God in spirit and in truth. We have, too long, let this pretense of spirituality pass muster for our best liturgical worship presentations to Almighty God.

So this work of research, editing, composition, and compilation is an attempt, on my part, to cull from the Methodist tradition in general, and "our own vine and fig tree" customs in particular, "that which is good, and with a breath of kindness, blow the rest away." Constructive criticisms and suggestions are asked of the readers, and the most enlightening of them will be considered for incorporation in any future revised printings.

It is hoped that the Stewardesses of our Zion will be willing to devote themselves exclusively to improving the scope and quality of a more reverent atmosphere in our Worship Services. May this manual be used as a guide in all such endeavors.

Still, after having said this, I must add this practical bit of sound advice:

In our denomination there are four ways to do things:

The right way;
The wrong way;
The A.M.E. way;
And your Pastor's way!!!

Your Pastor's preferences take priority over customs or manuals.

I want to express my deep appreciation to a former presiding elder, the Reverend P. Albert Williams, Sr., whose wise leadership in the Northwest Missouri Conference at that time caused the Liaison Committee for Stewardesses to be formed for their common enrichment in things "holy unto the Lord."

My most admirable appreciation goes to Mary Walker, Chairperson, Liaison Committee for Stewardesses, and a most knowledgeable layperson about the A.M.E. Church. She gave me sincere, profound, valuable assistance which has helped me in striving toward the mutual goal for reverent and proper liturgical worship throughout our Annual Conference.

Thanks to my brothers and sisters, who are yoked with me in the ministry, and who have shared their valuable wisdom and practical experience in a very comprehensive way to better my understanding of liturgical worship.

Special, loving words of thanks and dedication are for my very devoted and understanding wife for her encouragement when my weary, long, and sometimes frustrating sessions at the computer keyboard (way over into the midnight hours) would almost cause me grievous woe. Her loving support was just what was necessary to keep me going on so that this labor of love for our Church could be properly prepared and published. May God bless you my dearest.

Thanks be to God the Father, Son, and Holy Spirit for strengthening me to still be His servant in times like these.

Reverend Richard J. Parker
June 27, 1987

Preface
(Revised Edition)

Since writing and distributing the original edition, response to this manual has been better than expected. Many Pastors, Stewardesses, and others, have found it a useful training guide for local church Stewardesses, and ministry, even in the C.M.E. and A.M.E. Zion denominations. Suggestions have come to my attention which I have incorporated into this revised edition. Additional materials have been added, mostly in the Appendices, and the typeface has been upgraded to enhance readability. I send out this manual again in the hope that it will one day merit recognition by the Connectional Church, as a factor in producing more loyal and dedicated Stewardesses; and, indeed, a more enlightened clergy and laity.

Reverend Richard J. Parker
Kansas City, Missouri
May, 1988

Section 1

The Stewardess Board

The Stewardess Board

Purpose

The Stewardess Board exists to assist the Minister and the Steward Board, and is always under their direction.

Caring for God's House, keeping it beautiful and immaculately clean, is not only a duty, but also a privilege. Between the place where the paid caretaker's work stops and the Minister's work begins, there is opportunity for many expressions of loving service.

The Board could well take as its motto the much quoted saying of John Wesley: "Cleanliness is next to godliness," remembering that we manifest externally, by punctuality and cleanliness, an inner spirit of loyalty and devotion.

The nature of the Board's work make this auxiliary peculiarly the right arm of the Steward Board and the Minister. All members chosen should be women who have an understanding and appreciation of the meaning of congregational worship, or at least an inner urge to cultivate that interest.

The work of the Board is a sacred trust, and calls for women who are consecrated to the task, and who are willing to place love for Christ above personal feelings. It calls for women who are willing to work in the background, without recognition or praise from the congregation, for the most successful among its members is the one who is most self-effacing and inconspicuous in her work.

Should there be a constant difference of opinion between the Minister and a member of the Stewardess Board, the member should conform to the Minister's wishes or resign from the Board.

Organization

Multiple Boards--The *Discipline* states "The preacher in charge may nominate one or more Boards of Stewardesses. . . ." If this is the case in your local church, then a schedule of rotation on a monthly or seasonal basis would provide for a back up system for all services and duties, so that no Stewardess shall serve more than two weeks, including the Sundays, during the month (assuming the Board is large enough for such purposes). This would also allow for the busy modern day schedules which make such a system desirable, since it allows the members to have some "free" time when they are not on duty.

There should be some provision, moreover, for selecting new committee chairpersons periodically so that many members may gain the various experiences of that office.

Joint meetings for sewing bees, study and/or fellowship purposes would make for a spiritually cohesive group, other than just coming together on the first Sunday for Holy Communion, be that as important as it is.

Officers and Committees--The Board needs but a minimum of organization, but of course any group must have some sort of organization in order to function smoothly. A President, Vice-President, Secretary, Treasurer, and Chaplain should be chosen every year after the Annual Conference, and the reorganization of the local church's official board.

Some Boards organize the membership into separate committees, or pairs of members, to handle various responsibilities. These committee persons could be appointed by the President when the needs of the Board demand. The committee assignments may be deemed necessary as follows:

A Linen-Parament Committee is responsible for the repair, cleaning, and acquisition of paraments and linens. Some Boards sew their own liturgical needs.

An *Acolyte Vestment Committee* does the same work for the cottas and cassocks the Acolytes wear. These can be handmade also.

A *Chancel Committee* regularly cleans the chancel and its furnishings, cleans and polishes the metal ware fixtures, replaces candles, and does whatever is needed.

A *Flower Committee* schedules donations of memorial, or remembrance floral arrangements for each Sunday and for special days; potted plants as lasting memorials, are also quite acceptable.

A *Sacristy Committee* (or at least two persons) is responsible for seeing to it that the Sacristy is kept clean, and also taking special care to see to the return of all items to their proper places.

A *Sacraments Committee* makes ready all things (linens, vessels, Elements, candles, paraments, etc.) that are to be used to perform the sacred rituals in the church, and for the Love Feast; and/or Maundy Thursday Celebrations.

The Funeral and Wedding Committee (or else two separate committees) readies all the items for these celebrations.

When accepting the assignment for a specific month or week, the importance of faithfully and meticulously performing each of your duties should be carefully emphasized. *Nothing but your best and most wholehearted efforts can be acceptable in your work as a Stewardess.* No corners should be cut in carrying out even the smallest and seemingly unimportant aspects of your duties.

The Junior Board -- The *A.M.E. Discipline* states that "there shall be appointed a Junior Board of Stewardesses, who shall operate under the direction of the Pastor and the Senior Board of Stewardesses; there shall be a training course under the supervision of the Pastor and Senior Stewardesses." This is vital to the ongoing life of the church, that young people shall be trained to take the place, in the church, of homegoing saints.

The Junior Board can be young *ladies* (and I use that word advisedly), from 18 years of age through 25 years old, married or single, who have made a firm commitment of faith in Jesus Christ. They shall serve under the sponsorship of a full Stewardess for their training in all aspects of their duties.

They should all be similarly uniformed, but with black, lace Prayer Caps for a head covering until they are finally inducted as full-fledged Stewardesses, and capped with the headdress of the Board they are joining.

Acolytes--Some churches have Acolytes, youth who are between the ages of 10 through 17, who assist the Minister in leading the congregation in worship each Sunday by lighting and extinguishing the Altar candles, receiving the Missionary offering, picking up glasses from the worshipers at Communion, assisting the Pastor in Holy Baptism, and other services. The Pastor has the privilege of selecting and training these youths and encouraging their spiritual growth and development.

The Stewardess Board has the responsibility for seeing to the furnishing, care, and cleaning of the Acolyte's wardrobe. There should be a sufficient supply of different sizes needed, of the best quality possible, and there should be a long term plan for their replacement, when needed due to wear.

The cottas and cassocks may be easily made by capable persons on the Board. A person should be selected from the Board as Chairperson. She and her committee should see to it that the Acolytes are correctly and neatly robed each time they serve; that the Acolytes are trained in hanging up their cassocks and cottas, and that they are clean and neatly groomed.

Outline of Duties

1. To care for the Altar and the space in the Sanctuary which is enclosed within the Chancel area.

2. To prepare the Elements for the services of Holy Communion, Holy Baptism, and Love Feasts; and appropriately tidy up the Chancel area after the Service.

3. To care for, polish, and store all Altarware (candles, Holy Communion vessels, candle lighters, etc.), and appropriately, neatly store paraments, vestments, Baptism, and Communion linens.

4. To care for, polish, and clean the Baptismal Font, and provide its fine, white linen covering for it, provide shawls and/or towels for the Baptism.

5. To make provision for flowers and greenery for the Chancel, and candles for the Altar.

6. To change Altar paraments to the proper seasonal color.

7. To give advice, and propose church regulations concerning the Chancel arrangements for any special services, or ceremonies such as weddings, funerals, or candlelight services, when requested.

8. To assist in the worship service as needed, such as receiving new members into the church, lessening the discomfort of members, visitors, and clergy, and attending the deceased layperson's casket.

9. To assist the Pastor in delivering Holy Communion to the sick and shut-in persons, and on rare occasions, Holy Baptism, also.

10. *All Stewardesses* shall be in full uniform, and in their proper places at every Holy Communion celebration, as a whole group.

Helpful Suggestions

1. *At least two members should always work together.*

2. Begin all work with prayer.

3. Always wear work gloves (and dress gloves as the occasion requires) to prevent leaving finger and handprints on the Altarware and other Chancel fixtures.

4. Become thoroughly familiar with the Order of Worship so that you do not have to be prompted in your duties unnecessarily.

5. Attend study sessions given on the Church Year, Symbolism, Liturgy, and other phases of your work, which the Pastor, District Conference, or your Board may conduct from time to time.

6. Communion linens should never be sent to a commercial laundry, but should be carefully hand laundered, or washed in a good automatic washer. It is better not to fold linens after ironing. Instead, they should be rolled, without wrinkling, on cardboard tubes. Preferably, do not use starch.

7. If the candles have burned down to about 2-3 inches, replace them with new candles. On the 1st Sundays, or other Holy Communion days, or special days such as Christmas, Easter, weddings, funerals, Baptisms, etc., use fresh candles.

8. Altar paraments and vestments should never be folded, but rather hung carefully, without folding if possible, in the Sacristy, with dust covers over them.

9. Complete all your work preparations before any of the congregation assembles. Remember that

all your work should be as inconspicuous as possible.

During Invitation--Upon the announcement of the invitation to the congregation by the Minister (to accept the Open Door of the Church, and to become a lively member of the same) immediately following the Sermon, two Stewardesses, or a Deaconess and a Stewardess, should take their places in front of the Chancel rail, right and left, and remain standing facing the congregation until the indication that the Invitation is over. Return to your pew.

You should assist in receiving those who accept the Invitation, and/or who may be under the excitement of the Holy Spirit, in whatever way possible, and proper.

At the Parsonage--Inquire frequently as to the needs of the Pastoral family. The Board should assist in providing for the Pastor's table comforts and linens, especially at times of the hosting of Conferences, when the Pastor and wife may have to entertain many visiting Church dignitaries. The Board should provide help in the parsonage with cooking, serving, cleaning, and hostessing, along with other auxiliaries of the church who are expected to help also.

When a new Pastor is to arrive with his family, the Board, in consultation *and actual help*, with the Trustees and Stewards, shall see to it, among other things, that the Parsonage pantry and refrigerator have a few days provision in them to ease the transitional period of the moving of the Pastoral family.

Worship Attitudes and Etiquette

The Standing Position: shows respect in giving God praise.

The Kneeling Position: is the normal position one assumes in humble and petitioning prayer.

Bowing: used especially when singing the *Gloria Patri* ("Glory Be to the Father"), as a mark of respect.

Walking: never walk directly in front of the Altar without halting, and facing it briefly with a nod, or a bowed head.

Talking: never talk in front of the Chancel rail. Bring talk to whisper, and to a minimum in the Nave. Better still, NO TALKING--the Narthex (front entry area of the church) and/or the Fellowship Hall has been designed specifically for that purpose and use.

The Stewardess Garb

There is not now any Disciplinary ruling concerning the Stewardess uniform as there once was. Be that as it may, uniformity, simplicity, and modesty should be observed in matter of the Stewardess' Garb.

Each Stewardess Board should vote on their choice of appropriate attire, and receive the final, approving consent of the Pastor, and then each Board member should strictly abide by the regulations.

A white dress design that will be able to accommodate almost every member's fitting requirements should be chosen. Suitable, but similar modest head covering, hosiery, and white gloves.

Whether purchased or handmade, the dresses should be of the same material and general pattern for all Board's members. There is nothing more beautiful and inspiring in the church worship services, than the appearance and presence of well, uniformly attired Stewardesses. Conversely, nothing does more to distract from the dignity and inspiration of Worship than ill-clad, unkempt, or variously attired Stewardesses.

On other Sundays, or times when you are not scheduled for duty, wearing your uniform is optional unless the request of the Pastor is otherwise; or the dictates of your own conscientious faith urges you to always come attired in your Stewardess uniform.

All Stewardesses, however, should be in full uniform, and in their proper places at every Holy Communion celebration to partake of the Lord's Supper.

Ostentatious jewelry *should not* be worn while in uniform; no outlandish *baubles* on the ears, or *bangles* on the wrist or ankles, *or beads* around the throat should adorn those who at any time may be engaged in such a sacred duty as Stewardesses undertake. Wedding and/or engagement rings, which are symbolically suggestive of the mystical union between Christ and His Church are appropriate, all other rings should be removed.

Makeup should not be overdone, nor perfume overbearing. In the service of the Lord always remember who you are, and Whose you are. Don't ever enter into the service of God looking or acting like the Devil.

Section 2

The Christian Liturgical Symbols

CROSS SECTION OF A CHURCH

The Liturgical Symbols

Symbolism of Church Architecture

Methodism embraces a two-fold tradition of worship, the free and the liturgical, each making its own rich contribution to the life of the Church. We find these two aspects of worship reflected in two types of church architecture. In our denomination there are many variations between the extremes of these two types, and some of our A.M.E. churches combine features of both.

There is one characteristic which most houses of worship have in common, however. That is the division of the church into two parts; the Nave, where the congregation sits; and the Chancel, where the clergy are seated, and in its Sanctuary section, the Altar is placed, and the choir loft is located.

The meaning of the word *Nave* is "ship." It reminds us of the fact that the earliest symbolism associated with the church is that of the ship. It probably goes back to the thought of the Ark, and the Church, in comparison, being the "Ark of Safety," it was natural that the early church buildings were in the form of a ship. Indeed, the word

Worship is a combination of two words, "worth" and "ship," and implies that as the one who was chosen to be the Captain of the ship was "worthy of the ship," so the One whom we worship is worthy to be in control of our lives and of the universe. The act of our worship is our acknowledgment of that fact.

In order to be able to better interpret symbolism in our A.M.E. churches which are built along liturgical lines, let us consider some of the other strictly liturgical churches. For instance, the Lutheran and Episcopal churches have more uniform plans for their buildings, and more definite teachings concerning the symbolism which has been incorporated into the teaching of the Church over long centuries of Christian worship.

We find it often helpful in the study of Church symbolism to visit some of these churches. Perhaps we might now put our imagination to work and join a group in a make believe visit to such a church.

As we turn into the churchyard and up the steps and through the door, that in itself is a symbolic act, for it represents the turning aside from a life without God to a life of fellowship with Him through faith in Jesus Christ.

One of the first objects we see after entering the church is the Baptismal Font, which is placed near the door, symbolizing that it is the first step into the new life.

As we pause inside the door, we see ahead of us the broad, open aisle leading all the way to the other end of the church and ending at the Altar, and as we look over the building and try to become familiar with its details, we find our eyes going back to the Altar, and we can readily see that every item in the building is so arranged that everything directs one's attention back to the Altar.

We start down the aisle--or perhaps we should say up the aisle--for at intervals there are ascending levels and steps leading upward until we reach the Altar. We notice that the carpet is worn in some places, and it reminds us of the many people who have walked this way--young couples to take their marriage vows before the Altar, funeral processions, members of the church family who go to the Altar for Baptism, or to give their gifts, tithes, and offerings, or to offer prayers, or to partake of the elements of the Holy Communion, or for dedication vows.

Then we remember, as we walk from the doorway of the church to the Altar, that it is symbolic of the journey through life, from birth to death, always leading us to the presence of God. The steps leading upward remind us that our journey through life should also be ever upward.

The church has three parts (in this imaginary church tour)--the Nave, where the congregation sits; the Chancel, which is occupied by the minister and choir; and the Sanctuary in which the Altar is placed. Three steps lead from the Nave to the Chancel, one more from the Chancel to the Sanctuary, and three additional steps to the Altar. This makes seven in all, and seven is considered the perfect number, and symbolizes the transition from this life to the heavenly life. The three steps leading to the Altar represent the Trinity, and indicates that it is only through faith in the Father, Son, and the Holy Spirit that we have access to the sacred meal called the Lord's Supper.

The different parts of the church have meaning too. The Nave represents the Church militant, or the Church in this world; the Chancel represents the Church Expectant, or those who have passed into the life beyond, and the Sanctuary represents the

Church Triumphant, or the Church at the end of the age when our Lord shall reign forever. As we reach the Sanctuary, we find a kneeling rail, separating the Chancel from the Sanctuary, but with the center left open, for nothing is ever placed in the way of our access to the presence of God which is symbolized by the Altar. We learn that the end of the church, where the Altar is placed, is always designated as the "East" end, regardless of the actual direction.

This has an interesting bit of symbolism behind it, which had its origin in ancient Sun-worship. When the Sun-worshiping Gentiles were converted to Christianity, it was easy for them to comprehend the thought of our Lord as the "Sun of Righteousness," and they continued to worship with their faces toward the rising sun in the east, but with an entirely new meaning to the act, and with an entirely new SON!

We learn that the Altar symbolizes the Throne of God, and also serves as the Lord's Table. Its position indicates that God is the center of all our worship, and the entire service of worship is directed toward Him. The music, scripture reading, prayers, offerings (which symbolize the sacrifices of the people, and as such, are properly placed on the Altar when it is not adorned for the Lord's Supper), and the sermon, are the congregation's method of offering their best to the Highest we know.

All the Chancel furnishings are placed so as to help direct the attention of the worshipers toward God. The lectern is on one side of the Chancel (usually the left side, as one faces the congregation), and the pulpit on the other, at the outer edges.

The lectern, with the Bible resting on it, is for the reading of the Word, and the pulpit is for the preaching of the Word. The organ and the choir are also on the sides. The choir does not face the congregation because their purpose is not to give a concert, nor to entertain, but to take part in the service, to assist the pastor in leading the people in worship.

We must bring our visit to a close, although we have not covered nearly all the symbolism of the building. There is the bell, as it proclaims God's priority in our lives; the spire pointing upward to the one, true God; or the tower, symbolizing God as our Refuge and Protection. Then there are the stained glass windows which are rich in symbolism;

and the carvings on the pulpit and elsewhere. We begin to realize that our appreciation of the church will be much greater as we learn to "read" the symbolism of all that has been built into it.

Since our A.M.E. churches vary in form, all of these symbolic features may not be found in A.M.E. churches built on liturgical lines. The church WILL, however, be Altar centered, and the whole plan and arrangement will be to direct the attention of the congregation to the Altar, and to the One whom the entire service is our offering of penitence, praise, thanksgiving, witness, instruction, and self-sacrifice and self-dedication.

Altar and Chancel Appointments

The Cross: We use the Latin form of the Cross which is the oldest and most basic in design. There are over 50 distinct variations of the Cross. As Protestants, we do not use the Crucifix, which bears the body of Jesus, for our belief, of course, is that Jesus left the Cross and ascended on high in victory and triumph.

The Cross may be placed on the Altar, or on a Retable shelf on the back portion of the Altar, raised and centered; or on the wall in back of the

Altar. The Cross should never be used for decoration and should be limited, at most, to the two mentioned above.

The Candles: If used on the Altar, there should be only two in number. The candles should be lit for every liturgical (purely worship) service. The candles may be burned within three inches of the holders before they are changed. Holders should always be kept cleaned and polished at all times.

Beeswax candles should be used if at all possible. Candles symbolize Jesus Christ, the Light of the world. When one candle appears on each side of the Altar, they represent the two natures of Christ--human and divine. Six candles on each side of the Altar signify that our worship is never complete, and they may also represent the attributes ascribed to the Creator: wisdom, majesty, power, love, mercy, and justice; or they may represent the six days of creation; or the six hours that Jesus hung on the Cross.

If branch candelabra are used at all, they should be on the Retable shelf, or, better still, floor candelabra set inside the Chancel on either side of the Altar. A seven branched candelabra refers to the perfect life of Jesus, but mainly they refer to the seven gifts of the Holy Spirit: wisdom, faith, healing, miracles, prophecy, discernment, and tongues.

The Paraments and Linens: Should be of the best quality and workmanship that the church can afford, and cared for with the best attention. Linens must immediately be washed, and preferably not starched. Old linens should be reverently burned.

The Baptismal Font: It is the vessel through which the first Christian Sacrament is administered. It should never be neglected or abused, and should always remain in its appropriate place inside the Chancel area. It should only be filled by a Steward, Stewardess, or Acolyte, preferably, or by the Minister.

The Christian Flag: It signifies Christianity in its entirety-- faith, worship, traditions, responsibilities, and all of its blessings. The Cross on the flag symbolizes the Christian faith--God's love for His people and the promise of eternal life. The blue background speaks of the faithfulness and sincerity of the Savior, who was obedient unto death. The white portion of the flag is symbolic of the sinlessness of Christ.

The Altar: Methodists consider the Chancel area to be "the Visible Word," and that it speaks silently, and yet loudly, spiritually. We consider, also, that the Chancel may convey in its way, when the Word is not being preached, a proclamation of the Word as effectively, and as profoundly, as any number of words. This message is powerfully reinforced when the worshipers see before them visual evidence that there are people who "care enough to give their very best."

The Christian Year

The calendar for the Christian year is a means of teaching the events in the life of Christ and keeping them before the people. There is need for an orderly and balanced presentation of the Gospel story, and the teachings of Christ, especially to the children and youth. Each generation must learn anew all of the great truths of the Bible, and all of the events of the life of our Lord while He lived here on earth.

The Church calendar, and the plan of the Church year, with its seasonal hymns, Scripture readings, colors, and symbols, provide a framework through which the teachings of the Church can be given in an orderly and rhythmical manner, instead of being left to individual impulse. During the year every part of the Christian faith is given due emphasis.

Every great event in the life of our Lord is brought to our remembrance, and we experience anew His birth, His ministry and teachings, His death, resurrection, and ascension. During the long season of Pentecost (or Trinity), and Kingdomtide, the Gospel truths are presented from various angles for our spiritual nourishment and growth. The plan of the Christian year has proven such an instrument of spiritual growth that surely it must have come through divine guidance.

The plan of the Church calendar insures the witness of the *whole* Gospel. Each person in the Trinity is honored, and His Holy Office work is emphasized. Every event in the life of our Lord is relived in such a way that it becomes not only an event in history, but a present reality.

During the different seasons of the Christian year we feel the entire congregation should be aware of the messages and meaning which the colors and the seasons symbolize. When the hangings are changed from one color to another, it is not because of a "whim," or a "yen" to redecorate. They are not used merely for their beauty and decoration, but to arouse in us a remembrance of sentiments and dispositions in keeping with the season being observed.

The Seasons of the Church Year

1. Advent--Season of expectancy, looking toward the coming of Christ; includes the four Sundays preceding Christmas Day.

2. Christmastide--Season of Nativity; celebration of the birth of Christ, which includes Christmas Day, and the two Sundays leading up to Epiphany, or Twelfth Night (the 6th of January).

3. Epiphany--Season of the Evangel, which celebrates our Lord's outreach to the Gentiles. Epiphany Day is the celebration of the presentations of gold, frankincense, and myrrh to the Christ Child, by the Three Wise Men. Four to nine Sundays are included in this season, depending on the date of Easter.

4. Lent--Season of Penitence and Renewal, symbolized by our Lord's forty day wilderness vigil in preparation for His ministry.

5. Eastertide--Season of Resurrection, beginning with Easter Sunday and continuing fifty days, the biblical time between the resurrection and the day of Pentecost.

6. Pentecost (or Trinity)--Celebrates the coming of the Holy Spirit to the apostles, fifty days after the resurrection. Early it became known as White Sunday, when Baptism was administered to the new converts who were all robed in white. This season includes Trinity Sunday, the first Sunday after the day of Pentecost (the birthday of the Christian Church), and extends over eleven to sixteen Sundays, depending on the date of Easter.

7. Kingdomtide--Season of Teaching emphasis, which begins with the last Sunday in August (the Festival of Christ the King), and extending to fifteen or sixteen Sundays to the beginning of Advent.

Colors In the Church

Color has always been used to denote meaning to life. So the use of varying colors in the paraments (Altar cloths, Pulpit and Lectern scarves, and Clergy stoles) is an added means of symbolizing truths of God to the people. If only one color is used, red or maroon is to be preferred, with the addition of white for Holy Communion and, perhaps, weddings and festival days. The ideal preference would be to use the full five colors as follows:

Purple--which signifies royalty in the coming of the King in the Advent Season; in penitence, watching, self-denial, and self-discipline of Lent.

Green--which speaks to us of nature, growth, and life; used for Epiphany and Kingdomtide Seasons.

Red--symbolizes blood, fire, and Christian zeal, used appropriately, for the Pentecost (or sometimes called Trinity) Season.

White--the color that signifies "without spot or blemish," adorns the Chancel on Easter Sunday and during Eastertide; on Trinity Sunday; on All Saints Day; on Festival of Christ the King Sunday; on Christmas Day and the first and second Sundays after Christmas; on the first Sunday after Epiphany Day; and, in the A.M.E. Church, on all Holy Communion celebrations.

Black--the color of mourning; used only on Good Friday, if at all.

Flowers In the Church

Flowers are always found in churches throughout the world, for they represent the beauty of God and the resurrection of Jesus Christ. Their exquisite beauty and variety of shapes and colors make them truly an offering of praise and thanksgiving to the Father.

It is easy, however, to misuse their beauty, so a few basic rules should be followed when preparing them for use in the church. Two principles must certainly apply.

First, is the location--where or in what part of the church they will be placed.

Second, is the occasion--If it is a Festival Day, a wedding, a funeral, a regular service, etc.

The Altar should never be crowded with flowers, so as to obscure the Cross. Use pedestal tables on either side of the Altar preferably, and be sure that the flower's tallest branch is no higher than the arms of the Altar Cross. They are not to be used in front of the Cross unless the Cross is elevated completely above the tallest part of the flowers. Nothing should obscure any part of the Cross, nor should the floral arrangements be so showy as to detract from the Cross in any way.

The occasion for the floral arrangements is most important. Christmas, Easter, and Thanksgiving are our most important festivals and we should make our places of worship as glorious and abundant with flowers and greenery as funds, good taste will permit.

Traditionally, we do not use flowers during the Advent or Lenten Season, except on Sundays and Maundy Thursday.

Christmas permits lavish use of the traditional greenery and poinsettias, carnations, roses, or any other seasonal flowers, in red or white if desired, make a magnificent display.

An abundance of Palms are, of course, most appropriate for use on Palm Sunday. There should be enough of them to make an outstanding display, since no further flowers are used.

Easter, traditionally, calls to mind white lilies, and they are most often used. However, other spring flowers may be used to good advantage also. Here again we strive for a truly outstanding display of flowers, greenery, and palm branches to celebrate this most important day in the Church Year.

Thanksgiving is one occasion that seems to demand an Altar arrangement of the cornucopia of fruit, vegetables, grains, and flowers. It is a most appropriate time to symbolize our offerings to the Lord for all that He has given us. While the arrangement can be as large as good taste and design permit, we must remember the primary rule: *Nothing in front of the Altar Cross unless the Cross is elevated, and, of course, no part of the arrangement can obscure any part of the Cross.*

Since flowers symbolize the resurrection, it goes without saying that *no type of artificial flower or plant should ever be permitted in the Nave, Chancel, Sanctuary, or any other place in the church where people gather for strictly worship services.*

It is also imperative that no flowers or plants be allowed to remain that have begun to wilt. They should be removed at once, and empty vases should never be left on the pedestal tables, Altar, or in the Chancel area.

Better still, if the Nave is not going to be used by worshipers attending services for an extended period of time during the week, then give the flowers to the sick and shut-in to enjoy unless, of course, the donor wishes to have them for personal giving.

Potted greenery or plants that are permanently on display in the Chancel area should be given periodic and proper watering, pruning, dusting, cleaning, and polishing so that they may be kept looking fresh and alive.

Section 3

The Sacraments

The Sacraments

The A.M.E. Church, as do all Methodist denominations, recognizes and performs two Sacraments--Holy Baptism and Holy Communion. These were ordained by our Lord and have always been observed in all Christian churches. There is great spiritual strength to be found when we participate in these Sacraments, realizing that our Lord did so Himself, as well as Christians ever since.

The total commitment that we make during the Sacramental observances must necessarily lift us to a higher plane of living. Stewardess Board members should, therefore, approach the preparations of these two services worthily--that is with humility, reverence, and deep love for Christ, our Lord, and His Church.

A Communion Steward is usually appointed by the Pastor, and serves at the Pastor's pleasure, and that Steward acts as liaison person between the Steward Board and the Stewardess Board, seeing to it that whatever is needed to aid the Stewardesses in their labors of love will be cheerfully provided.

Following is a detailed outline for the preparation for the observances of the Sacraments. These procedures have been traditionally and precisely worked out and should be followed to the letter, thereby eliminating any guess work, and relieving the ministers of any surprises during the Service.

Holy Communion

Preparations--Holy Communion is usually celebrated on the first Sunday of each month at the morning Worship Service. It is also often observed on special occasions, such as Maundy Thursday (the evening before Good Friday), Easter, World Wide Communion Sunday, Christmas Eve, or on New Year's Eve. Sometimes Holy Communion is provided for the Bride and Groom only at weddings. Check with your Pastor for his preferences concerning these and other special day observances.

When Holy Communion is observed at Worship Services, other Ministers, the Stewards, Stewardesses, Acolytes, or Deaconess may assist the Chief Celebrant Minister, as his wishes require. It is the Stewardesses, however, who bring clean, tepid water in a lavabo (bowl), and clean, white lavabo towels for the washing and drying of the Celebrants' (Clergy's) hands.

Communion linens are cared for as a sole responsibility of the Stewardess Board. Laundering of all "Fair Linen," as often as needed, is done by capable members of the Board. Hopefully, all Communion linens can be used more than once before laundering becomes necessary, but if unsightly spotting occurs, laundering done right away will help keep the linens looking fresh and immaculate.

White paraments are always used in the Chancel area for Holy Communion celebration in our denomination, regardless of the color the Season calls for. The Altar railing is draped from end to end, and the pulpit is completely draped (and lectern, too, if there is one). The Baptismal Font is usually only draped for Holy Baptism observances, if the Minister so wishes.

Holy Communion vessels are to be stored in loosely fitted, dust proof, gray flannel bags (which capable persons can make) to maintain their luster and beauty. After each use, the Communion ware is all polished with Glass Wax. If you use silver trays, etc., always wash them with mild detergent, or wipe with liquid silver polish (according to directions), rinse and dry, and then store them safely in the flannel bags.

Used Communion glasses are washed in very hot water and detergent, rinsed in very hot water, dried to remove any spots, and stored in covered plastic containers. The amount budgeted for wine, bread, cleaning and laundering supplies, etc., is provided by the Steward Board, or the Stewards shall reimburse the Stewardess Board for their full expenses. Most Boards have an Annual Day to help raise sufficient funds for the yearly needs.

Preferably, instead of store bought Communion Wafers, homemade, unleavened bread may be used. It is becoming a lost art to make it, but the recipe for it, and the manner of preparing it, is given later on in these guidelines. If you are fortunate enough to have a senior Stewardess on your Board who knows the art, be sure you get her to teach the rest that it may be passed on to your posterity.

Dust and polish the Altar, all Chancel furniture, and Altar railing, before properly placing communion linens and paraments in their proper places in the Chancel area.

Fill Communion trays with cups and pour juice, about 3/4 full. Each tray holds about 40 cups. The filled trays are placed in one stack in the center of the Altar, consisting of the tray base, as many trays of filled glasses as needed, and the tray cover.

Place Communion wafers, or unleavened bread, on a bread tray and cover with another empty tray, placed upside down, or with a bread tray cover. If neither of these items is available to you, cover the bread with a clean, white, opened linen napkin that will completely cover the tray. Place only enough bread on the tray so that it will not readily fall off. Wrap some extra bread in a small, clean, white napkin and place in back of the bread tray for consecration with the other bread, in case additional bread is required. Place the bread tray beside the trays of filled glasses, according to the Minister's preference (left or right).

Neatly wrap the bottle, or Flagon, of remaining Communion wine that will be left over after all the glasses needed have been filled in a clean, white, linen napkin and place it on the opposite side of the trays of filled glasses from where you placed the bread tray. This is so that the remaining contents of the Communion wine can also be consecrated during the Ritual, in case additional glasses of wine will need to be poured during the Communion Service to accommodate the communicants.

Cover the entire Altar, with all the above items *neatly* placed on it, with the "Fair Linen" cloth so that a minimum of folds will be seen. It must hang evenly and straight on all sides of the Altar.

Worship Service Procedures--The Stewardesses should take their stations to fulfill their assignments immediately after the Call to Christian Discipleship (in "The Order of Worship") without waiting to be told. One or two Stewardesses should be prepared with a bowl of tepid water and clean towels for each of the Clergy Celebrants to wash and dry their hands after the Chief Celebrant has extended the invitation to Holy Communion.

Some Ministers allow the Stewardesses to uncover the Altar before the beginning of the Ritual, after the hand washing of the Celebrants. Most Pastors, traditionally, feel that no one should be inside the Chancel area that surrounds the Altar during the most sacred moments of Holy Communion celebration, except ordained Clergy and Acolytes assisting in the Ritual along with the Chief Celebrant.

If the Stewardesses are asked to perform this high privilege, the "Fair Linen" covering cloth should be very reverently and ceremoniously, without a great show or flair, removed by two Stewardesses, one on each side of the Altar, and folded by both, so that finally, when the cloth is placed in an open space to one side of the Communion vessels, it will be in the form of a triangle, symbolizing the presence of the Holy Trinity (the Father, the Son, and the Holy Spirit).

After this function is performed, then *do not approach the Altar, inside the Chancel area, again until you are ready to tidy up after the Worship Service is over, and most of the congregation has left.*

Stewardesses are not to remove the tray covers for the wine and bread. This is to be quietly removed with the fingers of both hands by the Chief Celebrant only, without clanging them against the trays, and the wine tray cover placed on top of the folded cloth triangle.

The cover for the bread tray (Paten), or the folded napkin, is quietly placed by the Chief Celebrant in an open space on the Altar near the Paten.

Some Pastors prefer that female communicants' heads be covered while partaking of the Lord's Supper. They explain that since the Stewardesses and Deaconesses are to have their heads covered while attending to their privileged duties in the Worship Service, and working about the Altar and Chancel, it is implied, and a matter of scriptural respect to God, that females should have head coverings. There is no strict law concerning this in the Church, just tradition and/or pastoral preference.

If your Pastor wishes it, then cover each grown female communicant's head with a delicate, white lace prayer cap as they kneel at the Altar rail, and remove the caps after they have finished drinking the Cup, before arising.

During the Holy Communion portion of the Worship Service, the Stewardesses and ushers are responsible for conducting, in a dignified and orderly manner, all who come to the Altar for Communion. Stewardesses will direct all prospective communicants to the Altar rail, after they have been ushered from their pews by way of the outer aisles.

Be ever alert to be of assistance in every way-- directing them to open spaces to kneel, holding the ladies' handbags till they are finished, and then return them; assisting with the small children, and the physically handicapped in particular (chairs offered if needed, or support while standing, if required)**; aiding those who may be momentarily filled with the conviction of the Holy Spirit; collecting empty glasses (unless this act of kindness has been assigned by the Pastor to someone else); directing those returning to their seats by way of the center aisle, and any other thing that will further enhance the beauty of the Worship Service.

****Note**: The custom of some churches of taking the Holy Communion Elements to the pews of those who are handicapped, in no small way robs that prospective communicant of the spiritual dignity of their personhood. Many such individuals feel that if Christ could make it to Calvary, under the handicap of carrying His own Cross, then certainly they can make it to the Cross of Christ at the Altar, since they have, at least, made it into His Church to have Supper in remembrance of Him.

Traditionally, the Stewardesses are served last, as a whole group by themselves (so every Stewardess ought to be present, in uniform, whenever Holy Communion is observed), by the hand of their Pastor or Chief Celebrant only, as a gesture of thanks for the tender, loving service Stewardesses render through their church to God the Father, Son, and Holy Spirit.

After Service is concluded, remove the Elements from the Altar; pick up any dropped Consecrated Bread or larger pieces of Bread crumbs and dispose of them by strewing them reverently upon the outside grounds. Remember, the crumbs are not garbage and should not be thrown in the trash can. Remove the Holy Communion vessels and used Communion glasses and give them a proper cleaning and carefully store them away. Any Consecrated Wine remaining in them should be given to the Pastor for his uses; or stored in the refrigerator of the church for future use; or reverently poured upon the ground from where it once came. Remember, it too is not sewage, and should never be poured down the drain. Under no circumstances is the Consecrated, Holy Communion Wine to be consumed like a commercial beverage by the Stewardesses as they clean up.

Remove the linens, Chancel furniture and Altar rail hangings, and other paraments and store them properly as instructed. Change the Chancel paraments to the appropriate color for the Season. Even the tidying up should be done with as much reverent decorum as possible. Leave the Sacristy clean and neat, no matter how you found it.

For the Sick and Shut-in--If you are asked to accompany the Pastor to deliver Holy Communion to the sick and shut-in, the following preparations are to be made before, during, and after the visit, as the case may be. If the Pastor has a Communion kit (if not, it would certainly be a gift the Pastor would treasure from the Steward and/or Stewardess Board), be sure that it is clean and the Elements of Communion replenished.

Upon entering the room, cordially greet all present and go about your duties. Unfold a white linen napkin, large enough to hold the vessels from the kit, and place it upon a nearby table in view of the persons who are to take communion. The Pastor will ascertain how many you are to prepare for.

Some Communion kits are more elaborate than others. Some have two small candles affixed in the cover; and plush lining with a cross embroidered in the center of the cover; and silver cups, tray, and bread receptacle (Pyx) with a cover that can be used as a small tray for the Communion bread. Become familiar with what the present Pastor has and be able to quickly, and efficiently prepare as he engages in conversation with the worshiper. Open the kit and remove a sufficient number of Communion glasses, and the Communion bread receptacle. Pour each glass 1/2 full; make sure sufficient Communion bread is available, but do not break any into pieces, the Minister is supposed to do that.

Allow the Minister to handle the elements as he would at the church Altar, for in fact the prepared place is the Altar in these instances. When all is ready alert the Pastor that he may proceed.

Take your position, in an attitude of worship, to the side. Join in the General Confession; sing along with the Minister in the familiar hymns, recitative prayers and Scriptures, if used.

When the ritual is finished, ask the family if you may wash the glasses. Wash them in very hot water and wipe them dry with paper towel as if polishing them, and replace them in the kit. Wipe any other vessels used and store them in the kit.

Reverently fold the napkin, upon which the kit was set, and if there is room, store it in the kit as well. Quietly close the cover securely so it won't accidentally open, spilling the contents.

Bride and Groom--Usually a single Chalice and the Paten are used. About one-third of a cup of the

Holy Communion wine is poured into the Chalice, and two wafers (or pieces of unleavened bread) are placed upon the Paten.

If there is no Chalice available, then use two Communion glasses and place them on the Paten with the bread and cover as above. Of course, these preparations should be done before the people begin to assemble for the ceremony.

Then center these items on the Mensa of the Altar in front of the cross, and cover with a clean, white, fine linen napkin, with a cross embroidered on it. Usually the napkin is given to the couple as a remembrance of the day they took their vows together.

Although the custodian is responsible for cleaning the areas used by the wedding party, after the ceremony has ended, the Stewardess Board is responsible for seeing that the Sacristy is left in good order; that all candle holders and candle lighters are cleaned and refilled. Also, make sure you have changed the Chancel paraments to the correct color, especially so if it is a Saturday wedding.

Recipe for Unleavened Bread
2 cups sifted 100% whole wheat flour
1/2 teaspoon salt
6 tablespoons cooking oil
1/2 cup cold water

Sift flour again with the salt. Blend oil and cold water together and pour over flour. Mix flour, oil and water and form into a soft ball of dough. Knead the dough a few times and roll it out to a *very thin* crust. Place on a flat cookie sheet; score with the dull side of a table knife to make approximately 150 rather small squares; and bake in a moderate oven (350-375 degrees) until *golden brown*.

NOTE: *Do not use yeast or baking powder.* Crust may also be rolled to fit in a large skillet and cooked until *lightly browned*.

(Recipe provided by the courtesy of Mary Walker)

Holy Baptism

Worship Service Procedures--These preparations, as with all the Stewardesses' work, are to be done before anyone assembles for the baptismal ritual. Sometimes the Minister may determine that a baptism is to be done in private because of extenuating circumstances, but most generally, and preferably, it is a public ritual, that eloquently speaks to the witness of the faith we have, that is for all the world to see.

The paraments are not changed for Holy Baptism, whatever color the season calls for is to be left as it is. Some Ministers prefer to have the Font draped in white, as well as the Altar railing.

One Stewardess will stand by each family with infants and/or small children, or person who is a candidate for baptism, to perform the necessary preparations for the actual moment of baptism, as quickly (without a show of rushing) and as dignified as possible.

Other Stewardesses will have handmade, white linen capes or baptismal towels ready to drape about the candidate's shoulders.

Sprinkling--Put about one quart of fresh, warm water into the metal bowl of the Baptismal Font and replace the Font's cover. Use any clean, appropriate bowl instead if no Font is available. The small white lavabo towel, to be used to dry the Minister's hands, is to be held by an Acolyte or Stewardess.

Use the baptismal towels and gently wipe the heads of those who have been baptized while they are yet kneeling at the Altar, or being held in the arms of the Minister, in the case of infants and/or small children.

The consecrated water remaining in the Font after the ritual is finished should not be allowed to stand unduly overtime because the evaporation will warp the wood and corrode the metal of the Font. As soon as is expedient, after the service, the Consecrated water should be emptied upon the outside grounds, reverently. The bowl is washed and, if it is metal, wiped with a soft cloth that has a small amount of mineral oil on it in order to keep its luster.

Pouring--In the case of baptism by pouring on of water, large, white, absorbent, baptismal towels are used to protect the candidates clothing, and to catch and wipe, as much as possible, the excess water from their heads. The water should be warm and placed in a large pitcher called a Ewer and not in the Font. Be sure you have enough water to be Consecrated all at once, for all of the candidates who are going to be baptized.

This mode of baptism is rarely used in our churches anymore, sprinkling is the much more preferred custom.

Immersion--For baptism by immersion, another Minister, or Steward, should assist the Minister doing the actual baptismal ritual. The Stewardesses will assist the female candidates to change to the appropriate baptismal garment, called Chrisom, in the dressing room, and accompany them to the pool (baptistry) steps, where the Minister and assistant will receive them and perform the rite. Stewards will do likewise for the male candidates.

After the baptism has been performed for the candidate, be ready to assist them from the top steps of the baptistry and lead them (some of whom may be under the excitement of the Holy Spirit), gently back to the dressing room.

Bear in mind that most of our churches do not have a baptistry in the church, so more than likely you will be a guest in a church that has opened its doors in Christian fellowship to you, your fellow members, and Pastor. Allow the women and other persons of that church to assist you in familiarizing yourself with the accommodations available to you for you to do your work. Be sure to take everything you will possibly need to accomplish your labor of love for the candidates, the Minister, and the assistants. Leave the areas that you used clean and tidy, regardless of how you found them.

For the Sick and Shut-In--You and your partner may have to accompany the Pastor to help with baptism of a person who is sick unto impending death, or a shut-in. The same above preparations are to be as completely carried out as circumstances will permit, and with the same reverence and tenderness. The rite will be administered by sprinkling, of course. If your heart is right, the Holy Spirit will give you the strength to carry out your duties with grace.

Section 4

The Celebrations

The Celebrations

Weddings

It is important that every couple preparing for a wedding in the church arrange for counseling with the Pastor as soon as possible, so that they may be made aware of your church's regulations for the use of the building, as well as the grounds.

Your Board should take time to prepare a pamphlet on the subject. Many hours of needless aggravation can be saved by acquainting the bride and her family, with regulations and suggestions contained in such a pamphlet.

A wedding consultant should be appointed from the Board, if there is such a person that is capable, or from the congregation. She should be one who will make herself thoroughly familiar with the church's policy and Stewardess Board practices and standards, and be able to tactfully advise with family members, caterers, and vendors concerning the proposed wedding plans.

The following quotation is taken from the *Manual for Methodist Altars*:

"The church should be made as festive and beautiful as it is possible to make it, but it should keep the atmosphere of a church--a House of Worship (remember that a wedding service is a service of worship and consecration)--a religious ceremony. The bride-to-be (if she decides to be married at the Altar of the church) certainly should make no attempt to change the church into a garden scene, or to move the furniture out to make room for an elaborate floral display."

The flowers, palms, potted greenery, and candelabra should be carefully placed so as not to hide the Altar, Cross, or Pulpit. As in all church decorating, everything should be arranged to direct the attention toward the Altar. The florist's awareness should be brought to the following guidelines as a matter of church policy.

No furniture may be moved without the Pastor's knowledge and consent.

Flowers--A self-supporting arrangement of flowers may be placed on both sides of the Altar Only greenery may be used behind the Altar. Nothing is to be placed on the Altar. Under no conditions will flowers or candles or greenery be placed between the Altar and the congregation. No flowers (or candles) are to be placed on the organ or piano without taking proper care to protect the wood finish of these instruments from damage by water, scratches, wax drippings, etc.

Aisle Cloth--The cloth runner spread down the center aisle in the church for weddings may not be fastened to the rug in any manner. Metal bars, wrapped in the color of the runner, may be used to anchor it at the front and rear.

Candles--All candles shall have receptacles, and in addition a mat of proper dimensions shall be placed on the floor underneath them to prevent tallow from dripping on the floor, furniture, or fixtures. This mat may be of paper, cloth, or plastic, but must not be unduly noticeable. Candelabra may be used if desire, if the same conditions are adhered to.

Prayer Desk (Prie Dieu)--a prayer desk for the bridal couple to kneel upon may be used.

Fasteners--No nails, tacks, pins, staples, or any other type of metal fasteners may be used on the furniture, carpets, floor, or woodwork in the church.

Home-Going (Funerals)

In recent times, people are having different thoughts about funerals, and in view of the many questions which are often asked, as in the case of weddings, the Board should have a pamphlet prepared as a guide for funerals. It should contain everything that the Minister and Steward Board have deemed necessary to make this occasion as comforting and easy as possible for the families involved. The Stewardess Board should become familiar with its regulations before it should be necessary to put them into practice. We quote again from our source manual, *Methodist Altars*, as one of the finest expressions available toward the proper use of the church.

"In no service of the church are flowers so *misused* as they are for funerals. Too often the deceased is only a small part of the service. The display of flowers is more talked about than the sympathy expressed on such a solemn occasion.

"Because there are people who like the custom of sending flowers upon the death of a loved one or friend, we feel that a word concerning the subject is important. Some families prefer flowers, while other families ask that flowers be omitted entirely, realizing that some people find the lovely thought of contributing money to a charity or medical fund in memory of the deceased more satisfying than sending flowers. In this way much more can be done to relieve the suffering of the world.

"The process of Christianization has kept pace in some areas of life, while in others we remain pagan."

Lying In State--It is quite appropriate, if desired by the family of the deceased, to have the body lie in state for viewing in the Narthex, or in the rear of the Nave, for a reasonable period of time immediately prior to the time of the scheduled funeral service. Those that arrive for the service walk by and pay their last respects to the deceased. This includes the family, who shall be the last to do so.

After the family has all entered the Nave and taken their seats, the casket is closed, out of sound and sight of them, and wheeled to the beginning of the aisle, where the Funeral Pall is placed upon it before it is escorted down the aisle by the family-selected Pallbearers.

The casket comes to rest at right angles to the Altar. The head of the deceased should be toward the congregation, unless the person was ordained, then the head is placed toward the Chancel area and the Altar.

Thanks be to God, more and more families are beginning to see the wisdom and spiritual significance, the beauty and the dignity of *not* opening the casket for a "review" after the benediction.

Funeral Pall--It is our recommendation, if the funeral is to be held in the church, that a pall belonging to the church be placed over the casket. Whether made of silk or other fine material, a Funeral Pall lends dignity and meaning to the service, for it symbolizes the great truth that all people are equal in the sight of God.

The Pall can be made of either purple or white material that is compatible to the other paraments. A large cross is usually the only symbol embroidered on it, recalling to us our belief in the resurrection and eternal life.

A floral Pall may be ordered by the family and used instead, but if the cloth pall is used, then it is suggested that a spray, or a double spray of flowers, be ordered to place on the casket when the service is over.

Do not place floral arrangements on top of the Funeral Pall.

The silk Pall is never to be taken out of the church.

When the silk Pall is used, it should be made available before the body arrives at the church. It is a good idea to spread the Pall out on a table to let the wrinkles fall out as is possible, touching up with an iron where absolutely necessary (using the ironing board). The Pall is then laid over the back of the last row of pews in readiness for the entrance of the casket into the Nave for the Home Going Celebration.

Great care must be exercised in the storing of the Pall because of its weight, size, and fine material. It should be carefully folded with tissue paper interleaved between the folds, and stored in an adequate amount of space to prevent crushing and wrinkling.

Duties--When the Board President, or Funeral Chairperson, is notified about the pending church funeral service, she should see that the following things are done before the service takes place. If she needs additional help, check the schedule and contact the weekly workers on the Board. The Funeral Chairperson is responsible for seeing that the Chancel and Sacristy are left clean and in good and proper order immediately following the Funeral, and the paraments must be replaced with the correct seasonal color.

Mourning Bows--Appropriately drape the pulpit for a clergyperson's death, for 30 days of mourning, with a black crepe bow, centered at the top.

For the demise of a Bishop, place a bow of narrow purple ribbon on the black bow as well.

For a General Officer, a pale blue ribbon bow, in addition, should be used.

If a Presiding Elder in your Conference has died, place a red ribbon bow on the bow as well.

A light grey ribbon bow is to be used if the deceased was a Minister or Pastor of your local church.

The same acts of mourning should be accorded the deceased spouses of any of the above also, when the occasion presents itself.

For a layperson's death, who was a member of your local church, drape the end of the pew for 30 days with a plain black bow on the center or inner aisle, near where they usually sat.

If the deceased layperson was a General Officer and held membership in your local church, then drape the pew end of the very front pew on the center or inner aisle, with a black and pale blue ribbon.

Laypersons, now deceased, who were members of your church, and who were also Connectional, or Episcopal District, Conference Branch Officers, or a Presiding Elder's District Officer, in your Annual Conference, drape the pew end, near where they customarily sat with a plain, black bow (except for Bishops, and other clergy spouses, and General Officers, use the proper ribbon colors as noted).

If your church feels so disposed to appropriately drape the pulpit or pew for those you hold in respectful remembrance, of any one of the above who may have been a former laymember, or pastor, of your local church, by all means do so. It will be a fine witness of the fact of our Connectional fellowship of love, one toward the other.

Parament Color--The purple paraments are always used for funerals. The Stewardess Board member in charge should see that they are placed on the Altar, Lectern, and Pulpit.

Candles--Check the candle holders to be sure they are clean, and the candles long enough to burn through the service.

Chancel Metal Ware--Polish the wax followers on the Altar candles if needed, and other metal ware as needed.

Processional--In the Funeral procession (into the Nave) of a Bishop, General Officer, Presiding Elder, or a Pastor, Stewardesses are paired with a Deaconess (or if none, then within their own ranks), and, led by their respective Presidents, should march directly behind the family, and be seated in a section opposite the family.

During the Service--If there is no one from a lodge or other organization to attend the casket during the service, two Stewards or Stewardesses should do so. One stands or sits at the head of the closed casket, the other at the foot. The pairs are rotated as inconspicuously as possible about every 15 minutes or so, except during prayers, Scripture reading, when the rotation takes place at the conclusion of these parts of the service. During the the Eulogy, the Preacher symbolizes the attentive honor being given to the deceased and no one else is needed to be at the casket. In addition, the Stewardess should be alert during the service to comfort any distraught family members or guests as the need arises.

Recessional--The Stewardesses serve in the recessional by holding the various floral displays that make up the passageway from the church building to the hearse, as the Pallbearers bring the casket for loading.

At the Graveside--Two Stewardesses should accompany the Pastor (and stand with him at the head of the casket) to assist him where needed, to hold his coat and hat, assist family members, and take the responsive part in the Committal Service as outlined in the *A.M.E. Discipline.*

Good Friday--The large, wall cross arms, in particular, (or the Altar Cross) should be appropriately draped with a piece of long, plain, black or purple crepe. Do so by noon on Good Friday until 6:00 a.m. Easter morning, when the crepe is to be removed (or before anyone arrives for the earliest worship service on Easter Sunday morning). Ask for the custodian's help to drape the wall Cross, and to remove it afterward.

No paraments of any kind shall be used during the above hours of mourning for our Lord's crucifixion on Good Friday. The Chancel and Altar shall be stripped completely bare of all ornamentation, appointments, and floral displays during this same period, except, of course, if you are using the Altar Cross in the act of mourning.

Love Feast Preparation

The Love Feast, as observed by the A.M.E. Church, is a modernized form of a very ancient spiritual custom. In the first days of the early church, Christians would assemble to talk about things concerning their new faith, and to meet with one another in love, friendship, and kindness. These meetings were not particularly times of worship, but rather social times for the family of God. During those times refreshments were served as a hospitality gesture.

From that type of meeting there grew up a custom of holding feasts at certain times at which neighbor Christians gathered in love and fellowship for spiritual stimulus. Those feasts were looked upon as most excellent things, since they brought Christians together as a family of love, promoting the cause of Christ, leading to conversions, strengthening the idea of the equality of all believers as members of the household of God. John Wesley revived the custom for his bands and classes and ever since it has been one of the usages peculiar to Methodists.

The Love Feast is held in many A.M.E. Churches on the Prayer Meeting night just preceding the first Sunday of each month, or whenever the Holy Communion is observed. Some of our churches have Love Feast as often as the Pastor may see fit. They are also often held just prior to the commencement of many of the Conferences of our Connectional, Annual, and District gatherings; and are open to all "other serious persons" who wish to take part, regardless of church affiliation. However, no food is generally eaten.

The ranking Minister or Pastor of the local church where the rite is being observed should preside. A small table is usually placed between the Chancel rail and the first row of pews in the Nave.

Upon it should be spread a clean, white cloth. Trays of bread slices that have had their crusts removed, and have been cut into 1/2 inch strips, are nicely placed upon the covered table, along with trays of communion glasses that have been filled with cold water.

Another clean, white cloth, large enough to cover the table and its contents, is spread over it before the rite begins, and again before anyone assembles.

When the song, prayer, Scripture, and testimony portion of the celebration has ended, then the Stewardesses assigned will uncover the table ceremoniously and with reverence.

After the observance has ended, the Stewards will collect the bread bits and crumbs from the members' hands, and put them on the trays where the Stewardesses will appropriately dispose of them.

Maundy Thursday Celebration
Paschal Lamb Feast

The Paschal Lamb Feast is a historical reenactment of the events in the Upper Room; the fellowship Jesus had with His disciples, during the Feast of the Passover, where He instituted the Last Supper. The Paschal Lamb (without spot or blemish) is symbolic of Jesus Christ who was to be offered up in sacrifice for the sins of the whole wide world.

In modern Judeo-Christian Tradition the feast is celebrated after sundown on the Thursday before Easter Sunday, and the Feast foods eaten are to bear a close similarity to those prepared and eaten in Jesus' day as is possible. The significance of the Feast will be spiritually filling, perhaps more so, than physically filling.

Prior Preparations

This event should be a joint effort of the Board of Stewards and Stewardesses, with all members of each board participating in all its aspects.

Reservations for the Feast, from your local church members first, then other denominational guests, should be received the week before Palm Sunday, so that ample space accommodations for tables and chairs, and enough food (especially the legs of lamb during the Lenten Season), paper goods and supplies, etc., can be ordered well in advance. In order to minimize confusion, there should be no overflow of guests. Everyone invited should have a seat. Take into account guest clergy couples, the choir, or other singing group, or soloists and musicians. No charge is to be made for the event. The sacrificial offering, received during Worship should cover the expense.

The Stewards and Stewardesses shall set up the fellowship hall with sufficient tables and chairs, in the form of a large cross, well before the appointed time the event is to take place. Other tables can be placed, *neatly*, around the room, near the large cross tables as space will allow. The chairs shall be placed on both sides of all tables, and at the ends. The end chair at the table forming the top of the cross is for the Pastor, and the other chairs at that table, and the three other end chairs (one at each cross arm end, and one at the foot of the cross) are for those who will be reading Scriptures, and/or visiting clergy. A pair of floor candelabra should be placed, one on each side, at the top side of the cross arms, in the "L" shape of the head cross tables. Additional votive candles shall be spaced on all the tables so that sufficient light is present. *Do not use electric lights.* A fairly large, low bouquet of flowers shall be placed at the center point of the head tables where the three meet.

Other Stewards and Stewardesses, meanwhile, shall prepare the foods, put place settings on the tables, dress the Chancel and prepare for Communion Service, etc. Family-style serving dinnerware may be used; however, the use of paper and plastic goods (table runners, napkins, cups, plates, serving bowls, forks, knives, and spoons, etc.) is high desirable, so as to minimize cleanup time *after the event is completely over.* The simple fare, and subdued ornateness, will also reflect on the manner of our Lord with His disciples in their day.

Every Steward and Stewardess shall take part in the Paschal Feast and the Holy Communion Service. The worship of God takes precedence over anything else. Members of both boards will serve the meal and should alternate turns during the meal so that all may eat and participate. There will be no talking among the guests, or members of the Boards. People desiring more food (they may eat as much as they wish) will point to it. Board members will have to be very alert to anticipate needs, to pass serving dishes down the table, or even between tables.

Menu Items

The meat should be purchased from a meat packer or butcher shop, or near wholesale. Get legs of lamb, boned, rolled, and tied; allow a minimum of 1/4 pound of boned meat per person when ordering. (This is symbolic of the lambs used in sacrifice in New Testament times.) Do not serve mint jelly with the lamb; use a minimum of seasoning in cooking; cook very slow for tenderness. The meat should be cooked, in ample time prior to the Feast, either in the church kitchen, or at various members homes. Slice meat thinly (by commercial electric meat slicer, preferably), and keep it warmly moist.

(Other food items may be purchased mostly from a store which has Jewish Kosher foods, if desired; make purchases in #10 hotel size cans, and in quantity lots to minimize costs.)

Watercress, or other exotic lettuce: separate the leaves and tear into medium portions. (This represents the bitter herbs.)

Matzos (Kosher, unleavened crackers): break into smaller pieces.

Olives: black or green; with pits left in.

Canned Figs, Kadota variety: drain liquid off.

Dates: pits left in; separated.

Almonds: whole, unblanched (brown nut meat husk left on).

Canned Tangerine, or Mandarin Orange slices: drain liquid.

Wild rice: cook so grains are separated, not mushy.

Water to drink; in paper cups; no ice. (Kosher wine may be used).

Place all food items in appropriately large type serving dishes, or on platters, and place very conveniently at several places on the tables; allow a grouping of food items for each 5-6 people. No condiments, salt or pepper are to be placed on the tables.

Format

1. Congregation, and other participants, assemble in the Nave at the appointed hour after sundown (or 6 PM, taking into consideration daylight savings time, work hours, etc., to maximize participation); quietly, without whispering or conversation, and meditate. The Stewardesses assigned to prepare for Holy Communion shall have done their

work well ahead, and be in uniform for the service. Other Stewardesses, also uniformed, and some Stewards, will be putting final touches on the serving of the Paschal Feast.

2. The printed Order of Worship is followed (see Appendices). All persons will process, at the proper time, without talking (but singing, *Let Us Break Bread Together*) to the fellowship hall.

    a. If two Acolytes are used to lead the procession, they will light the candelabra upon entering the Hall, otherwise, two Stewards will light the candelabra and the table votive candles on the tables when they hear the procession approaching. The Acolytes shall sit facing the Pastor, one on each top side of the "L" formed by the cross arms.

    b. Ministry will seat themselves as stated above; Choir and/or soloists sit at reserved tables near the piano; Congregation will sit wherever space is available; both Board members sit at reserved tables nearest the kitchen.

3. After everyone is seated, the Pastor, or designate, will read the proper Scripture lesson, and the Lord's model Prayer will be prayed in unison. Then the eating begins. The feast will then be further conducted by the Pastor according to the Holy Scrip-

tures sheet prepared for the ministry (see Appendices). A small bell, such as is used in the Sunday School, will be placed at the Pastor's chair, who will use it to alert the ministry and singers of their time to participate at various intervals throughout the Feast. One ring, for Scripture readings to commence; and two rings for music. Everyone will remain seated, and eating may continue, during the reading and singing. *No talking to each other during the entire Feast.*

4. At the end of the Feast, which should last about 20-25 minutes, all will rise; and, led by the choir, Acolytes, Ministry, and Stewardesses, will proceed to the Nave, without speaking, as before, and then continue the Order of Worship and Holy Communion, after receiving the Offering.

5. After Service the Board members will return to the Fellowship Hall for cleaning up. Uneaten, edible food can be divided among the Board members in an appropriate manner.

Section 5

Additional Information

ACOLYTE
 ALTAR
 CASSOCK
 CELEBRANT
 CHANCEL

 CHALICE
 COTTA
 DOSSAL
 EWER
 FLAG, CHRISTIAN

 FLAGON

 FONT

 PALL, FUNERAL
 LATIN CROSS
 LAVABO
 PATEN
 PRIE—DIEU

 NARTHEX
 NAVE
 RETABLE
 STOLE
 SANCTUARY

Definitions of Ecclesiastical Terms

Acolyte--A server; a lay assistant to the Minister, often a youth, one of whose functions is to light and extinguish the Altar candles.

Advent--The first season in the calendar of the church's year; it consists of the four Sundays prior to Christmas.

Altar--The Holy Table; the Communion Table; a place also for the offering of prayers and the giving of vows, and the presentations of the sacrifices of the Christian community (gifts, tithes, and offerings).

Ash Wednesday--The first day of the Lenten Season; it begins forty days before Easter, excluding Sundays in Lent.

Baptismal Font--The receptacle, finely made of stone, metal, or wood, which holds the water for Holy Baptism.

Baptismal Towel--A white cloth used for wiping the head of the baptismal candidate; it is often cut 18" x 22" but may be larger for use in baptisms by pouring or immersion; it usually has a cross monogrammed on it, and is often given to the candidate after the ceremony as a remembrance.

Baptistry--A large pool used for baptisms by immersion; constructed in a separate space near the Chancel area, supplied with running water.

Cassock--The long, black undergarment worn by the clergy and Acolytes, and sometimes choristers. There are two styles commonly in use, the Roman style, which is buttoned down the front; and the Anglican, which is buttoned down the side.

Chief Celebrant--The ordained clergyperson who is in charge of conducting the celebration of the Holy Communion; such as a Bishop, General Officer, Presiding Elder, or local church Pastor, or their designates, usually assisted by other ordained clergy.

Chalice--The common cup, most often very ornately made of metal, containing the wine distributed in Holy Communion; most used often nowadays in our denomination only for the wedding couple.

Chancel--The East End of the church, so called regardless of actual direction, raised above the level of the Nave by steps (or a step). In the A.M.E. denomination, technically, the area most usually between the choir loft (which is separated by a choir screen) and the Altar rail.

Chrisom--A white, robe-like garment traditionally worn during Holy Baptism by immersion by a candidate to signify new life in Christ, as a lively member of His Church.

Christmastide--The second most important festival (after Easter) of the church year because it focuses on the incarnation of our Lord. The cycle includes Christmas Eve, Christmas Day, one or two Sundays after Christmas, until the 6th of January; this season should not be allowed to supplant the resurrection celebration as the center of the church year.

Church--(a) The body (committed persons) of Christ; (b) commonly, the House of God; that building (the institutional, physical complex) set apart by formal dedication to worship Almighty God.

Church Year--The Christian year, arranged by the church for commemoration of our Lord's life and work, and for the great events in the history of the church; the organization of seasonal cycles, festivals, and occasions into an annual series; it begins each year on the first Sunday in Advent, the fourth Sunday before Christmas Day.

Communion Rail--A railing separating the Altar space and Chancel area from the Nave on one or more sides, at which communicants kneel to receive the Holy Communion; synonymous with Altar Rail, or Chancel Rail.

Communion Table--Literally, in our denomination, the table from which the Holy Communion is served at that particular time; the Altar.

Cotta--A white linen, waist length vestment worn by the clergy Acolytes, or choristers over the cassock.

Dossal--A fabric, usually of rich or ornate texture, hanging on the "East" wall behind the Altar; also known as the Dorsal Curtain; can be changed seasonally along with the other parament colors; if permanently installed do not duplicate any of the seasonal colors.

East Wall--The wall behind the Altar which is always referred to as the liturgical east wall, regardless of its true direction.

Eastertide--The principle festival of the church year, celebrating the resurrection of our Lord; a fifty day period of rejoicing which ends on Pentecost and includes Ascension Day.

Ecclesiastical--Relating to, or belonging to, a church, especially as an established institution.

Elements--The physical materials used in the Sacraments of Holy Communion and Holy Baptism (bread, wine, and water) to which God attaches His gifts of salvation, life, forgiveness, and membership in the Christian community, when they are properly administered.

Epiphany--Always celebrated on the 6th of January; it is symbolic of the Wise Men's appearance before the Christ Child, bringing gifts of gold, frankincense, and myrrh; the season may include as many as nine Sundays, depending on the date of Easter.

Ewer--A pitcher used to carry water to fill the Baptismal Font; used instead of the Font in the ritual of baptism by pouring.

Fair Linen--A "fine linen" cloth which is the principle covering of the Altar, especially during the celebration of Holy Communion; it is called "fine' or "fair" because it is 1) always made of the very best material the congregation can afford, 2) the object of the most scrupulous care, and 3) that Altar cloth upon which the finest embroidery is placed. In the A.M.E. tradition it is used to cover the Holy Communion vessels on the Altar that contain the Elements of Holy Communion. It is to be ceremoniously removed, usually by the Chief Celebrant and an assistant, and folded into a triangle, symbolizing the Trinity, and placed on the Altar just before the ritual is entered into.

Flagon--A large, covered glass or metal container used to hold the reserve portion of the Holy Communion wine.

Funeral Pall--A large cloth, usually made of silk and embroidered with a large Cross, centered from top to bottom and side to side; used to cover the casket during funeral services in a church; sometimes a floral pall is used.

Gloria Patri--A Latin phrase which means "glory be to the Father." *It is always to be sung with the head bowed.*

Lavabo--The small bowl that contains the water used for the rinsing of the fingers of the clergy just before the celebration of Holy Communion.

Lavabo Towel--A white cloth used by the clergy for drying the hands after using the lavabo.

Lectern--A stand, quite a bit smaller than the Pulpit, placed in the Chancel area on the left side (as one faces the congregation), on which a Bible rests and, traditionally, from which the scriptural lessons are read at worship services; unordained persons

Additional Information

may speak from the Lectern as the occasion requires.

Lent--The forty days of preparation and reconciliation prior to Easter. It begins on Ash Wednesday and ends in the special observances in the Holy Week just before Easter Sunday; it is a time of renewing the grasp one has of Christian teachings and self-sacrificing living.

Litany--A solemn responsive form of supplication.

Liturgical--The use of symbolism throughout the architecture, furnishings, appointments, worship services, rites, rituals.

Liturgy--A Greek word meaning "public service"; the Order of Worship, centered on Word and Sacrament, for including all persons in a common act of worship as they respond to the gifts and the presence of God, with faith poured out in praise, song, acts of love, and a life shaped, and lived, by the discipline of sanctification.

Love Feast--A devotional service, observed by Methodists, which precedes and is preparation for the partaking of the Lord's Supper.

Maundy Thursday--Celebrates the Last Supper

the Thursday evening before Easter, from Jesus' command to love one another.

Mensa--Latin term for "table"; the top surface of the Altar.

Narthex--The entrance area of a church building.

Nave--The portion of the church building between the Narthex and the Chancel, in which the congregation is gathered for worship; from the Latin word for "ship."

Paraments--A word used to designate the cloth hangings, linens, and vestments, in seasonal colors, and often displaying liturgical symbols, used to embellish the Chancel furnishings, mainly the pulpit, lectern, Altar; in the A.M.E. tradition this would also include the covering over the entire Altar rail as well; vestments of the clergy and Acolytes are implied.

Paten--A round plate, usually made of precious metals, used for serving the bread at the Holy Communion ritual.

Pentecost--Day of celebration of the birthday of the Christian church, the coming of the Holy Spirit, as the promised Comforter, for Jesus Christ's sake.

Prie Dieu--A French term for prayer desk, usually equipped with a kneeler and a shelf to hold a

Additional Information

prayer book; most often used, in our denomination, in weddings for the bridal couple, and/or in worship, during prayer.

Pyx--A small covered container in which is kept the reserve supply of Communion Bread to use during visits to the sick and shut-in.

Retable--A low step or shelf placed at the rear of the Altar upon which the Cross and candle holders are most appropriately placed; often called a "gradine," a Latin word meaning "step."

Ritual--A formal, transcendent, prescribed, symbolic, physical, long practiced traditional ceremonial act or action used in congregational worship.

Rite--The text of a liturgy combined with ceremonial action practiced in a denominational tradition.

Sacrament--In Christian practice, a worship act through which God gives His visible Word promise; Holy Baptism and Holy Communion are recognized as the only two required Sacraments of our denomination.

Sacristy--A room near the Chancel area where vessels and paraments used in liturgical worship are stored, and where the Stewardesses perform their maintenance and preparatory duties; also used as a place where the Clergy and Acolytes keep and don their vestments.

Sanctuary--In older church buildings the area in the immediate vicinity of the Altar within the Altar rail and the "East" wall; sanctuary is not the proper name to use for the church building.

Stole--A long, ornate, silk cloth strip, in liturgical colors, hung around the neck of ordained ministers only.

Tre Ore--A three hour service frequently held on the afternoon of Good Friday, from noon to 3:00 p.m., when the time is divided into a series of meditation on Jesus' seven last words from the cross.

Vestments--Distinctive liturgical garments worn by the Clergy and Acolytes as they perform their duties in the sanctuary of the church.

Wax Followers--Cylindrical, heavy fittings, usually made of brass, sized to the dimensions of the candles being used, firmly placed at the top of the candles to allow complete consumption of the wax by the flame as the fitting "follows" down to the bottom of the burning candle.

Reference Books For Further Reading

The Book of Discipline, the Bicentennial Edition, African Methodist Episcopal Church, AMEC Sunday School Union, Nashville, TN, 1984.

The Genius and Theory of Methodist Polity, or the Machinery of Methodism, Bishop H. M. Turner, D.D., LL.D.; Publication Department, AME Church, Philadelphia, PA, 1885.

A Guide Book for Deaconesses, Stewardesses, and Altar Boys, Reverend Charles H. Copeland.

A Working Manual for Altar Guilds, Dorothy C. Diggs, Morehouse-Barlow, Wilton, CT, 1983.

A Concise Dictionary of Ecclesiastical Terms, Reverend Frederick L. Eckel, Jr.; Whittemore Associates, Boston, MA, 1960.

United Methodist Altars, A Guide for the Local Church, Hoyt L. Hickman; Abingdon Press, Nashville, TN, 1984.

Pastor's Guide to an Acolyte Program, Phillip C. Peace; Abingdon Press, Nashville, TN, 1970.

The Elder at the Lord's Table, Thomas W. Toler; CBP Press, St. Louis, MO, 1985.

A Manual for Altar Guilds, Reverend Carl F. Weidmann, A.M.; Ernst Kaufmann, New York/Chicago, 1955.

Symbols of the Church, Carroll E. Whittemore; Abingdon, Press, Nashville, TN, 1984.

Appendices

Maundy Thursday Celebration

Order of Worship

[**Note:** ( ) = print instructions within the parenthesis in the bulletin; [ ] = bracketed instructions for participants, do not print in bulletin.]

[In the Nave]

Organ Prelude (please pass quietly to a seat without talking. As soon as you are seated, engage in silent meditation.)

Lighting of Altar Candles [by Acolytes, or Stewardesses]

Processional Hymn [optional if there is no choir]

Invocation

Choral Response

Congregational Hymn

Explanation of Paschal Lamb Feast [by Pastor]

Procession to the Feast (singing *Let Us Break Bread Together*) [Acolytes, Choir, Clergy, Stewards, Stewardesses, Congregation]

[In the Fellowship Hall]

The Paschal Lamb Feast (To be eaten in silence, talking to no one)

Recession to the Nave (silently) [Acolytes extinguish the Candelabra Candles, and lead recession of Choir, Clergy, Congregation; Stewards and Stewardesses extinguish table candles, after each table of persons joins recession; follow procession to the Nave.]

Presentation of Offerings (*All Things Come of Thee, O Lord*)

Choral Selection [or solo, etc.]

Meditation [or sermon]

Invitation to Christian Discipleship

Congregational Hymn

The Holy Communion Observance [Form Optional]

Doxology (*Praise God, From Whom All Blessings Flow*)

Benediction

Recessional [Acolytes, Clergy, Choir, Congregation]

Organ Postlude (Leave with silence, until outside the Nave)

Paschal Lamb Feast
Order of Feast and Holy Scriptures
[*Print* entire *Scriptures (or use Bibles) for* all *Clergy and/or Stewards*]
[After the candles have been lit and all are seated, the following continues]
Pastor: [Read St. Luke 22:14-18]
Unison: [The Lord's Prayer]
[Serving dishes are passed in silence; persons indicate what they want simply by pointing--allow about 3 minutes eating in silence, then proceed with the following, as eating continues]
Steward or Guest Minister: [Read Luke 22:24]
Steward or Guest Minister: [Read Luke 22:25]
Steward or Guest Minister: [Read Luke 22:26]
Pastor: [Luke 22:28-30]
[Allow 3 minutes silent eating time, then read as follows; eating continues]
Pastor: [Read Psalm 113:1]
Steward or Guest Minister: [Psalm 113:2]
Steward or Guest Minister: [Psalm 113:3]
Steward or Guest Minister: [Psalm 113:4]
Steward or Guest Minister: [Psalm 113:5-6]
Steward or Guest Minister: [Psalm 113:7]
Pastor: [Psalm 113:8]

Music: [acappela choir selection, or a solo--spiritual preferably; after the selection has ended, allow 3 minutes silent eating time, then read the following; eating continues]

Pastor: [John 15:1-2]

Steward or Guest Minister: [John 15:3-4]

Steward or Guest Minister: [John 15:5]

Steward or Guest Minister: [John 15:7]

Steward or Guest Minister: [John 15:8]

Steward or Guest Minister: [John 15:9-10]

Pastor: [John 15:11]

[Allow 2 minutes eating time, then read the following]

Pastor: [John 15:12-13]

Steward or Guest Minister: [John 15:1]

Steward or Guest Minister: [Matthew 5:17-18]

Steward or Guest Minister: [John 14:27]

Steward or Guest Minister: [John 14:30]

Pastor, Stewards, and Guest Ministers in unison: [John 14:31]

[Proceed silently to the Nave for the Holy Communion Service]

New Stewardesses Induction Ceremony

This ceremony should always take place at a celebration of the Holy Communion, when the entire Stewardess Board is always present. It should be held on a first Sunday, preferably after the first Quarterly Conference, when the new Steward Board shall have been officially confirmed by the Presiding Elder.

The Stewardess candidates should have also completed their six weeks training course, which shall have included two first Sundays.

Each candidate shall be properly attired, except without head covering. The headdress for each candidate, shall be held by the Stewardess Board sponsor of each candidate. The President will have on hand a pair of fine white gloves that will be given to each candidate to put on at the proper time in the ceremony. Copies of this ceremony shall be made available to all participants.

Immediately *preceding* the Pastor's invitation for all communicants to "draw near" the Lord's Supper, the Holy Steward (if there be one appointed), or the Liaison Steward to the Stewardess

Board, and the Stewardess Board President, and the candidate(s) for induction (properly and uniformly attired), come forward, with copies of the ceremony in their hands, stand at the Altar rail, facing the congregation. Other members remain seated.

The Pastor shall say: **"Blessed are those servants whom the Lord, when He cometh, shall find watching." Let us all pray the Lord's Prayer together.**

The Lord's Prayer in unison.

Pastor (to the participants): **Let us recite the following Litany responsively.**

Pastor: **O Lord, send out Thy light and truth that they may lead me.**

Response: **And bring me unto Thy holy hill of Thy dwelling.**

Pastor: **And that I may go unto the Altar of God.**

Response: **Even unto the God of my joy and gladness.**

Pastor: **Glory be to the Father, to the Son, and to the Holy Spirit.**

Response: **As it was in the beginning, is now, and ever shall be, world without end. Amen.**

The Steward Board Liaison Steward (Holy Steward) steps forward.

The Liaison Steward Speaks: **Brother Pastor, I present to you these persons to be received into full membership in the Stewardess Board of this Church.** (Reads each name.)

As each name is read, each candidate turns and faces the pastor.

Pastor: (Addressing the President of the Stewardess Board). **Have these persons served their probation well and been diligent and reverent in the performance of their duties?**

President: **They have.**

Pastor: **Have they shown by their own personal devotion and regular worship that they are fit persons for this great privilege?**

President: **They have.**

Pastor (to the candidates): **What is your wish?**

Candidate: **I wish to serve as a member of the Stewardess Board of this Church.**

Pastor: **Do you promise to serve faithfully and devoutly, in any and all of your duties as member of this Board?**

Candidate: **I do.**

Pastor: **Do you promise to do your best to fulfill all of your obligations as a member of the African**

Methodist Episcopal Church and as a communicant member of this church?

Candidate: I do.

Pastor: While you kneel, let us pray.

All Candidates kneel

Pastor: O Lord, Jesus Christ, who didst accept the ministry of faithful women during Thy earthly life, we pray Thee to accept and bless the work which these women are about to undertake in the care of Thy House and Worship, Thy Word and Holy Sacraments, and preserve in purity and holiness their souls and bodies as living temples of Thy Presence, to whom, with the Father and the Holy Spirit, we give praise and honor, now and forever.

Lord, we beseech Thee, grant us grace to withstand the temptations of the world, the flesh, and the devil, and with pure hearts and minds to follow Thee, our God, through Jesus Christ our Lord. AMEN.

The candidates remain kneeling as each sponsoring Stewardess stands behind her own candidate, with head covering in hand. The Pastor receives the head covering for each candidate, and places it on the candidate's head.

The Pastor says to each one: **I welcome you and admit you into full membership on the Stewardess Board of this church. May God ever bless you.**

The new Stewardesses stand, together as one body, and then turn and face the congregation.

The hymn "Jesus Keep Me Near the Cross" is sung; the Stewardess Board President presents each new member with their own pair of gloves, which they immediately put on. All Stewards and Stewardesses give the new members a warm acceptance gesture, then all return to their pews.

Requirements and Equipment of the Sacristy

The following equipment and requirements are identified to assist the Board to determine its own needs for effective functioning within its particular space limitations.

1. *Large work surface.* A 3 ft. by 5 ft. table, or longer, for adequate handling, ironing, and pressing of linens and fabrics, and the many communion utensils.

2. *Sink and towel drying rack.* Hot and cold water for sanitary and careful cleansing of communion vessels, as well as obtaining baptismal water for the font; and for arranging flowers for display.

3. *Hot plate.* For superheating water to use in wax removal; or if there is no hot water piped into sink.

4. *Cabinet with full length mirrored door.* To be exclusively used for personal grooming articles; vestments for Acolytes; closet for the Board.

5. *Small Refrigerator.* To store communion elements for freshness; to save candles from warping or sticking together; and to keep flowers fresh.

6. *Storage space, Closet Spaces*, with covered racks for rolling, and hanging, of altar linens; covered rods for Acolytes, and baptismal vestments. *Long, shallow drawers*, to allow paraments to lie flat. *Smaller drawers*, for preparation utensils, gloves and other small items. *Cupboards*, for cleaning supplies for metal vessels and chancel appointments, fabric supplies, baptismal towels and shawls, tools, etc.

7. *Storage for precious items.* At least a strongly locked cabinet, to store communion vessels made of precious metals, and other items used in liturgical worship.

8. *An executive's corner.* Small desk, chair, and bookshelf, for use of Stewardesses reference manuals, liturgical books and Bibles, and a small bulletin board to post schedules, future events or services, and notices.

The following list contains items frequently used by Stewardess Boards. Experience will tell the local board which of these items may be most necessary or not. Consider carefully the care and storage requirements of these items.

1. *Wedding equipment:* kneeling pillows for bride and groom, candelabra, small communion chalice and paten.

2. *Funeral equipment:* funeral pall, flower stands, mourning bows, candelabra, if used.

3. *Decorating Supplies:* flower vases, arrangement frogs, trivets, seasonal appointments (cornucopia, Christmas creche, Advent wreath, and other liturgical decorations, palm fronds, Good Friday rough hewn wooden cross, etc.), fabrics, banners with wire, small rods, hanging cords, etc.

4. *General repair supplies:* assorted tools, scissors, knives, scrapers, nails, screws, thumbtacks, cup hooks, etc.

5. *Steam iron, ironing board.*

6. *Sewing equipment:* sewing machine, yardstick, straight and safety pins, various threads, buttons, etc. (to repair vestments, linens, etc.).

7. *Altar and other candles:* extra wax followers, candle discs to catch drippings, candle lighters and wicks, matches, protection mats or pads for vases and candle holders.

8. *Cleaning supplies:* detergents, dish cloths and towels, basins, pots or saucepan for superheating water (especially useful in removing wax),

large waste basket and plastic bags, metal polishes, stain removers, furniture polish (for chancel woodwork and furniture), small vacuum cleaners, supply of rags, and paper towels, napkins, and kleenex.

Care and Cleaning of Chancel Furnishings
Care of Paraments and Linens

The heavy fabrics usually used in paraments require storage in flat drawers. If folded or hung they become warped or worn at the creases. Since cleaning need not be done too frequently, it usually is best done by a professional dry cleaner able to give these fabrics the proper care.

For very ornate paraments, atmospheric conditions and long use on the altar can prove to be problems. Various fabrics may stretch or sag apart. Flat storage can help, but constant temperature and humidity will also be factors. Sewing a fabric liner on the backs of the paraments helps preserve the original appearance of the fabric.

Linens require relatively frequent laundering. The traditional, pure linen fabrics are best laundered by hand or in a *very gentle* machine wash. Mild soaps are most effective. Occasional bleaching--*but only in the sun*--will help forestall the linen's tendency to yellow with age. The same advice applies to synthetic or blended fabrics. Professional laundry equipment is almost never gentle enough for Altar linens, even for modern fabrics. Very expensive blended fabrics have been known to wear rather quickly under the stress of frequent commercial laundering. Experience also indicates that commercial pressing is rarely as satisfactory as hand work done by the dedicated members of the Stewardess Board.

Pressing and storage of linens must be done carefully. Linens must lie as flat as possible on the altar to prevent mishaps. If the edges of the linens tend to curl from ironing, they should be pressed on the wrong side. Avoid the practice of linens being folded and creased when pressed, to prevent curling. Storage on rollers is helpful, especially since it is usually impossible to provide long enough drawers for flat storage of the fair linen.

Treating Common Stains

The proper treatment of stains depends on the fabric and the nature of the stain. Church supply stores can give proper advice on these matters. Commercial spot or stain removers may also work. Only the most common methods of stain removal are given. *They may not be good for all fabrics.*

Wax is ordinarily removed from fabrics by laying the spot over an absorbent material (paper toweling works well). A hot iron applied to the spot will cause the wax to melt down and out of the fabric. If wax is heavily encrusted, scrape or chip most of it away before using the hot iron.

Wine, juice stains are common, especially in altar linens. Early soaking in cold water, followed by the usual laundering will take care of most stains. For more difficult stains a spot bleach, if not harmful to the fabric, may be used. Deep stains may also respond if rubbed with salt, after which the fabric should be laundered at high temperature.

Lipstick, often found on communion linens, will respond to spot soaking in most laundry detergents.

Perspiration and water stains may not come out of fabrics requiring dry cleaning unless the spots are washed with cold water before they dry. The water treatment, however, may badly affect some fabrics, and in that case there is no good method. Washable fabrics should pose no problem, but perspiration in garment collars and cuffs may have to be spot treated first.

Care and Cleaning of Metals

Like the fabrics used in the Chancel, the metals (usually brass) should be as clean as possible at all times. Allowing soot, wax, or tarnish to accumulate does nothing to reflect the presence of God among His people.

Wax or other dirt can be removed from brass by rubbing it with a soft cloth. Wax followers, however, often heavily encrusted with wax, may be put directly into hot water, allowing wax to float off. *Lacquered brass, however, should be cleaned only with wet cloths, then dried. Abrasives, hard scrubbing, or scraping are to be avoided lest the lacquer be ruined.* Unlacquered brass, on the other hand, very quickly loses its finish if handled with the bare hands. Gloves are recommended whenever handling such brass. Polishes must be used quite often on *unlacquered* brass to preserve their best finish and lustrous appearance.

Care and Cleaning of Wood

If the woodwork in the Chancel is not cared for by the janitor, it should be cared for by the Stewardess Board. They should assume all responsibility for cleaning and polishing as needed. This is especially important on pulpits and lecterns where hands frequently contact the woodwork. Some places on the Altar and Baptismal Font may also show results of frequent handling. Which polish or cleaner used will depend upon the type of wood finish. Avoid using water, since it eventually deteriorates the finish and raises the grain.

REGULAR DUTY CHECKLIST

Holy Communion
____ Chancel cleaned and in order
____ Linens & paraments in place
____ Candles replaced, if needed
____ Communion vessels ready
____ Lavabo, water, towels ready
____ Wine in proper quantity
____ Sufficient bread available
____ Pastor's Kit prepared
____ Baskets for empty cups
____ Women's head coverings
____ Other:
____ Other:

After the Worship Service
____ Linens treated for stains
____ Linens laundered properly
____ Paraments & linens stored
____ Vessels cleaned & stored
____ Wine stored for future use
____ Wine remaining from trays poured into earth
____ Bread from paten stored for future use
____ Bread strewn upon earth
____ Vestments, etc., stored
____ Other:
____ Other:

Other Worship Service Needs
____ Flowers properly arranged
____ Acolytes vestments prepared
____ Offering plates for Acolytes
____ Candle lighters ready
____ Other:
____ Other:

Love Feast
____ Table prepared and covered
____ Bread cut, covered
____ Water trays filled, covered
____ Table top cover placed
____ Other:

Weddings
____ Altar, etc., vested
____ Flowers arranged
____ Candle lighters ready
____ Special candles placed
____ Other:
____ Other:
____ Other:

Home-Going Celebration
___ Funeral Pall ready
___ Comfort supplies ready
___ Candle lighters ready
___ Candles replaced
___ Altar, etc., in Purple
___ Flowers arranged
___ Chairs for Honor Guard
___ Other:
___ Other:

Holy Baptism
___ Font cleaned, ready
___ Water in Font
___ Capes, towels, etc.
___ Immersion gowns, etc.
___ Drying towels ready
___ Water poured into earth
___ Supplies for sick/shut-in
___ Other: